D1713351

The Sam Walton Way

50 of Mr. Sam's Best Leadership Practices

Michael Bergdahl

50TH WALMART ANNIVERSARY
COMMEMORATIVE EDITION

Brighton Publishing LLC
Chandler, AZ
BrightonPublishing.com

The Sam Walton Way
50 of Mr. Sam's Best Leadership Practices

by

Michael Bergdahl

Brighton Publishing LLC
501 W. Ray Road, Suite 4
Chandler, AZ 85225
www.BrightonPublishing.com

Printed in the United States of America

Copyright © 2012
ISBN 13: 978-1-936587-48-3
ISBN 10: 1-936-58748-3

First Edition

Cover design by Tom Rodriquez

Cover Photo: Sam Walton, addressing the stockholders at the 1991 stockholders meeting in Fayetteville, Arkansas. (Photo Credit: UPI)

 *Review*

"Fast excellent read that serves as a reminder of what we should be doing."

"I just picked up "The Sam Walton Way: 50 of Mr. Sam's Best Leadership Practices" and I want to recommend this short read by Michael Bergdahl. When I took the Walton Institute of Retailing class, I saw that he is one of the suggested authors for further study. However, I've also gotten to know him through LinkedIn and was impressed at the way he leveraged not only his Walmart experience, but the experiences of current leaders and associates from his "Sam Walton's Best Practices" group to create a new, to the point, fresh take on Mr. Sam's leadership practices.

If you don't have a lot of time to read I'd still suggest picking this up, it breaks the best practices down into a "What Would Sam Do" format. Section one almost looks like a blueprint for our current stated focus: bench strength, accountability, empowerment, budget, focus. The "Focus" best practice reminds us to have one shared agenda: the customer. I think this is a book I'll keep around especially if I start to drag and need a 'pep talk'." (Amazon Reader Review 12-1-2011) **Clinton Plunkett, Supervisor Health & Wellness Center, Walmart**

ᴄ∕ᴐ *Dedication* ᴄ∕ᴐ

*To my wife, Sheryl, the best friend,
wife, mother and partner I could ever
have dreamed of. God bless you and
thank you for everything. You make me
a very lucky man.*

The Sam Walton Way – Michael Bergdahl

 *In Memoriam*

"I'd like to be remembered as a good friend to everyone whose life I've touched, as someone who has maybe meant something to them in some way."

Samuel Moore "Sam" Walton
(March 29, 1918 – April 5, 1992)

Presidential Medal of Freedom

On March 17, 1992, President George H. W. Bush honored Mr. Sam with the highest award bestowed by our nation on a civilian: the Presidential Medal of Freedom:

"An American original, Sam Walton embodies the entrepreneurial spirit and epitomizes the American dream. Concern for his employees, a commitment to his community, and a desire to make a difference, have been the hallmarks of his career. A devoted family man, business leader, and statesman for democracy, Sam Walton demonstrates the virtues of faith, hope, and hard work. America honors this captain of commerce, as successful in life as in business."

Presentation by
The Hon. George H. W. Bush
41st President of the United States of America

∽ *Contents: Section One* ∾

↪ *Contents: Section Two* ↩

ᕙ *Contents: Section Three* ᕗ

↶ *Contents: Section Four* ↷

◷ *Contents: Section Five* ◷

Preface

> *"If you love your work you'll be out there every day trying to do it the best you possibly can, and pretty soon everybody around will catch the passion from you – like a fever."*
>
> **Sam Walton**

On July 2, 1962, Sam Walton opened his first Wal-Mart Discount City Store at 719 Walnut Avenue in Rogers, Arkansas. In 2012, Walmart will celebrate its 50th anniversary. In recognition of Mr. Sam's fifty year leadership legacy I felt it was important to recognize this milestone.

Generations of Walmart Associates and Managers have come and gone, and few of those who are currently employed by the company actually knew Sam Walton personally.

To this day, Walmart's leaders continue to turn to Mr. Sam's leadership philosophies to guide them as they operate Walmart Stores and Sam's Clubs around the world.

This book, **THE SAM WALTON WAY**: *50 of Mr. Sam's Best Leadership Practices*, is a tribute to Mr. Sam, and it is designed to capture some of his best leadership practices for posterity, by asking and answering the question, "What Would Sam Do?"

I hope you enjoy this 50th year tribute to Mr. Sam's Walmart leadership legacy.

THE SAM WALTON WAY

Sam Walton was an ordinary man
Who started with a simple plan
His only dream to be the best
Not bigger, but better than the rest

His wife Helen was the one
Who helped Sam Walton get it done
When funds were tight in '45
Her father's loan kept dreams alive

Sam started with a single store
He never really wanted more
But as his idea gathered steam
His goal became a global dream

He imported goods from overseas
Manufacturing products for lower fees
He focused hard on lowering cost
His customers won: his competitors lost

He asked his customers what to buy
Then charged low prices and stacked it high
Thousands of customers shopped his store
With an insatiable desire to purchase more

His greeters smile and say hello
Welcoming customers they're sure to know
His Associates help and show the way
Providing great service every day

Sam made his customers number one
And shopping his stores was actually fun
Prices and products are guaranteed
And checking out is done with speed

He traveled here and traveled there
He flew his own plane everywhere
He visited stores across the land
Talking, serving and shaking hands

He believed his team to be the key
He gave credit to others for all to see
He was quick to diminish his own role
Crediting team success for achieving goals

His Associate partners meant so much
He treated them with a personal touch
He cared for them like trusted friends
And they believed in him until the end

"Mr. Sam" is the respectful name
Of this man who sought not wealth or fame
His legacy is the customers served
He'd say he achieved more than he deserved

Sam Walton was an extraordinary man
Who had passion along with a simple plan
He proved that dreams can come true
If you're willing to do what you have to do

by

Michael Bergdahl

Prologue

THE SAM WALTON WAY:
WWSD – What Would Sam Do?

Contrary to popular belief, Sam Walton wasn't born in Arkansas; he was actually born in Kingfisher, Oklahoma. He was raised in Missouri where he worked in his father's store while attending school. After graduating from the University of Missouri in 1940, with a degree in economics, he began his own career as a merchant when he opened and ran several Ben Franklin five-and-dime retail franchises. It would be more than twenty years after his college graduation before he opened his first Walmart Store in Rogers, Arkansas.

Did you know that when Sam Walton started his business he faced adversity that almost led to his failure? You see, he had an economic crisis when bankers refused to lend him money, and some of his product suppliers created a credit crisis for him when they forced him to agree to pay cash on delivery before they would ship products to his stores. His early competitors scoffed at his discounting strategies and poorly merchandised stores. It seemed everyone lacked confidence in his retail business strategy at a time when he needed to count on their support the most.

For Sam Walton to succeed, in those early and difficult days, took a singularity of focus, passionate leadership, and a never say die attitude! He had to overcome his own fear of failure and refocus himself on what to do to succeed. In the end he overcame all of those early obstacles, and the cynicism of all of those early naysayers, who incorrectly predicted his demise. Sam Walton had the last laugh as he grew his business from a single store to become the world's largest company. Along the way he also became the world's richest man! (Note: When he died, Sam Walton's personal family wealth was US$100 billion!) In the end, Mr. Sam transformed the way business is conducted around the world with his paradigm busting best leadership practices.

I was fortunate to have had the opportunity to work with, and around, Sam Walton, the founder of Walmart. That's how I learned that "THE SAM WALTON WAY" IS "THE WALMART WAY!" In this book, *THE SAM WALTON WAY,* as a tribute and to commemorate Mr. Sam's 50 year leadership legacy, I have captured 50 of his Best Leadership Practices. It is the foundation of his leadership that has led Walmart to become what it is today, the World's Largest Company. Interestingly, when faced with a difficult problem today's company leaders often find themselves still asking, "What Would Sam Do?"

When I worked for Walmart I worked at the home office in Bentonville Arkansas, where I had the unique opportunity to work with Sam Walton one on one. Every week I also had the chance to see him in action at Walmart's renowned Saturday Morning Meetings. These meetings provided me with unique first hand insights into his unusual leadership style that only an insider can provide.

Sam Walton had three basic beliefs that remain cultural anchors at Walmart to this day: 1) Respect for the Individual 2) Service to Customers, and 3) Strive for Excellence. These beliefs are practiced daily in interactions with customers, between store, distribution center, and home office team members. These three beliefs are also intertwined in all of Sam Walton's best leadership practices.

Sam Walton was a Servant Leader who never asked anyone else to do anything that he hadn't already proven he was willing to do himself. You might say he led by his own example. He taught his entire leadership team at Walmart to use *Golden Rule Values'* in their dealings with the *'Associates'* (Mr. Sam's term for employees). Sam Walton would often say, *"The Associates don't care how much their manager knows until they know how much their manager cares . . . about them!"*

In recognition of Sam Walton's love and respect for Walmart's more than 2 million employees around the world, I have capitalized "Associatc(s)" throughout this book.

One of the towering strengths of Sam Walton was his unique ability to gain the trust and support of the people around him. He called his customers "neighbors" or "guests" and he referred to the managers in his company as "coaches." He referred to the employees of his company as Associates or business partners and they referred to him, out of respect, as "Mr. Sam." In this book, out of respect, I too will refer to Sam Walton also as "Mr. Sam."

Deservedly, Sam Walton was included in TIME Magazine's list of 100 most influential people of the 20th Century. So what was it that made Mr. Sam so successful? What was it about him that led him to such monumental success? The basis of his success resulted from the fact that he was an entrepreneur with incredible discipline. He put his heart and soul into creating, nourishing, and growing his retailing empire. He spent every waking hour trying to make his company, and all of Walmart's people, the best in the world, and over time he succeeded. He was the most charismatic leader I have ever met, and he was also a very uncommon, common man.

So what did Sam Walton do that was so unique and unusual that made his company catapult to the top of the business world? Why is it that his competitors, suppliers, non-competitors, professors and college students across the globe study Walmart's best practices trying to gain insight into Mr. Sam's incredible success story? Why has his company continued to prosper while others have failed? To understand Walmart's success you have to understand the teachings of its founder Sam Walton.

To the outside observer, Walmart's high performing culture is one of the great mysteries of the company. The fact is the majority of Associates at Walmart really do care about their jobs and their company. They take tremendous ownership and pride in the Walmart Store or Distribution Center where they work. But why? It's not one thing it's many things. It's promotional opportunities and emphasis on teams. It's managers who care and fellow employees who are like a Walmart family. It's average people being given the opportunity few companies in America would ever offer to them. In the process, the Associates are motivated to achieve at above average levels of performance. Sam Walton admitted he was just an ordinary man who accomplished the truly extraordinary by working hard, maintaining the focus on his vision, and by inspiring the people around him to share his dream.

Sam Walton realized that people are Walmart's most important asset. He understood that by treating them as partners and empowering them to serve the customers he was unleashing a powerful business catalyst called ownership. Sam Walton was ahead of his time. He believed in the benefits of empowerment, continuous improvement, and ownership years before those concepts became the hottest program du jour, touted by business consultants around the world.

You might be wondering if Walmart still follows the teachings of its founder. I anticipated that concern by asking current Walmart Associates the question, "Does Walmart still embrace the teachings of Sam Walton?" Here is a sampling of the responses I received:

- *The company, to this day, continues to evolve and change the way I feel Mr. Sam was adamant about, in order for the success of his business.* Eric

- *Yes, indeed . . . without a doubt . . . and it is something I wish the "outside" world understood more about Walmart. Having worked around the world, I've never seen a company like Walmart and am extremely proud to be a part of its culture.* Rob

- *Since the first day I crossed the threshold, I have felt the special place that this is, and the good fortune that I now work with such an incredible team, family and company!* Connie

- *The Culture is ALIVE and well!! Just wish others on the outside would see and be open to what Walmart has done for not only their Associates, but families across the globe!* Ryan

- *Yes without a doubt, it's a part very essential in the fundamentals of Walmart; it's an important part in the operation.* Hugo

- *I think the fact that so much is still based on the 3 basic beliefs shows that Walmart is trying very hard to keep the teachings of Mr. Sam uppermost in everyone's mind.* Michelinda

- *I am proud to say that not only do I see our Associates practice Mr. Sam's teachings, and our 3 basic beliefs in the work place, but I also notice these teachings and beliefs practiced outside the work place in Associate's personal lives.* Tawfeek

- *I am incredibly proud and privileged to work for a company that is extraordinarily good at respecting its heritage and culture.* Dorothy

- *The company offers opportunity for growth; they give you a chance no matter your skin color. There is stability you don't have to live in fear of not having a job. It's busy and fast paced which makes working exciting and fun.* John

- *I am very proud of our culture and truly believe it sets us apart. Our focus should always be to not just learn and teach the culture but to use it in practice every day. All of us have a responsibility to be the 'Culture Keepers' of the company.* Tim

- *I think that Walmart still embraces the teachings of Mr. Sam overall. Most important is taking care of the Associates and they will take care of the business.* Bill

Mr. Sam's leadership philosophies, values, strategies, and tactics have remained the foundation of the Walmart culture for fifty years! In this book, **THE SAM WALTON WAY:** *50 of Mr. Sam's Best Leadership Practices*, based on my first hand observations and discussions with others who worked with Mr. Sam, I will review 50 of what I consider to be his most important "What Would Sam Do (WWSD), Best Leadership Practices." This book is "one stop shopping" for everything you ever wanted to know about *The Sam Walton Way*!

"The combined effort of all Associates to hold down retail prices, tightly control expenses, reduce inventory shrinkage, and improve productivity was the key ingredient in producing our record operating results."

Sam Walton

Section One

WWSD #1–SIMPLIFICATION:
Simplify everything you do
WWSD #2–BENCHSTRENGTH:
Promote from within
WWSD #3 ACCOUNTABILITY:
Maintain your standards
WWSD #4–EMPOWERMENT:
Empower your people
WWSD #5–ENTREPRENEURISM:
Think like a merchant
WWSD #6–FOCUS:
Have one shared agenda
WWSD #7–BUDGET:
Manage your expenses
WWSD #8–OVERACHIEVERS:
Above average results
WWSD #9–UNITY:
Internal service standards
WWSD #10–REINFORCEMENT:
Use folklore and storytelling
SAM WALTON'S THREE BASIC BELIEFS AND VALUES

❧ *WWSD: One* ❧

What Would Sam Do #1:
SIMPLIFICATION

At Walmart, Sam Walton believed in simplifying everything by embracing the "K.I.S.S." Principle (*Keep It Simple Stupid.*)

Simplify everything you do

Mr. Sam believed in simplifying every aspect of his business. For this reason, Walmart's success strategies and tactics were easy to understand yet hard for other companies to duplicate. This is because many business leaders have a tendency to value complicated solutions to problems, while discounting the value of simple solutions. Mr. Sam liked people to keep things simple, and that's what he taught Walmart's leaders!

What Would Sam Do #1:
SIMPLIFICATION

> *"The bigger Walmart gets the more essential it is that we think small, because that's exactly how we have become a huge corporation—by not acting like one."*
>
> **Sam Walton**
> (From: *Made in America*)

✎ WWSD: Two ✎

What Would Sam Do #2:
BENCHSTRENGTH

Out of necessity, Sam Walton often promoted Associates who clearly were not ready into jobs for which they had no prerequisite experience . . . and more often than not they'd succeed!

Promote from within

Sam Walton was a big proponent of promoting his own Associates to fill open management positions. He believed it was critical for new managers to fully understand the company's culture and the Walmart way of doing things, if they are to succeed. As a testament to his vision, seventy five percent of today's managers around the world were promoted into their current jobs from within the company.

What Would Sam Do #2:
BENCHSTRENGTH

> *"My role has been to pick good people and give them maximum authority and responsibility."*
>
> **Sam Walton**
> (From: *Made in America*)

 *WWSD: Three*

What Would Sam Do #3:
ACCOUNTABILITY

A large part of Sam Walton's success can be attributed not only to his ability to set high standards, but more importantly to his willingness to hold people accountable for reaching his lofty goals.

Maintain your standards

Mr. Sam respected people who set aggressive goals, but when they did he held them accountable for achieving them. He expected everyone around him to work hard and exert the maximum effort, but effort alone was not enough. The efforts of his team had to yield results. Mr. Sam set his goals high for the organization and he measured progress. Along the way he held his people accountability only rewarding those who actually succeeded.

What Would Sam Do #3:
ACCOUNTABILITY

> *"A promise we make is a promise we keep. High expectations are the key to everything."*
>
> **Sam Walton**

◡◠ *WWSD: Four* ◠◡

What Would Sam Do #4:
EMPOWERMENT

B̶y empowering his people, Mr. Sam gave every member of his team the decision making authority necessary to provide superior customer service without the need for management intervention.

Empower your people

Empowering people has turned Walmart's culture into a competitive advantage and the synergy created unleashes the organization's full potential. Mr. Sam pushed decision making down the organization giving local managers and

Associates the responsibility and authority to run their businesses and serve their local shoppers. By doing so, he was able to meet the specific needs of customers in communities around the world.

What Would Sam Do #4
EMPOWERMENT

> *"You've got to give folks responsibility, you've got to trust them, then you've got to check on them."*
>
> Sam Walton

☙ *WWSD: Five* ❧

What Would Sam Do #5:
ENTREPRENEURISM

Sam Walton made certain that everyone who works at Walmart was trained to think like a retail merchant, enabling every Associate to add value to the customer's shopping experience.

Think like a merchant

Sam Walton got everyone in the home office involved in selecting, promoting and selling products. His fanaticism for selecting just the right products and his enthusiasm for serving his customers is legendary. Leaders from Walmart's home office visit stores, speak to store Associates (employees), and talk with customers. Mr. Sam required all of Walmart's people to understand the business, the products, services, and the customer's needs too!

What Would Sam Do #5
ENTREPRENEURISM

> *"There's a lot more business out there in small town America than I ever dreamed of."*
>
> Sam Walton

⟪ *WWSD: Six* ⟫

What Would Sam Do #6:
FOCUS

S*am Walton inspired all of Walmart's leaders and Associates to focus on a shared agenda . . .*

The Customer!

Have one shared agenda

Mr. Sam demanded there would be only one agenda at Walmart and that was the retail agenda. Everyone from every department was required to think like a merchant and focus on the needs of customers. Mr. Sam expected everyone's primary job role to be a retailer first and whatever they did for the company secondarily. Imagine the power of so many people all focused in the same direction!

What Would Sam Do #6
FOCUS

"We need desperately to support, listen, and assist each other with the bottom line being to serve our customers better with quality merchandise at the lowest prices."

Sam Walton

✑ *WWSD: Seven* ✑

What Would Sam Do #7:
BUDGET

𝓜r. Sam was a tightfisted money manager who believed in constantly reducing costs and then passing the savings along to his customers with the lowest priced products.

Manage your expenses

Sam Walton changed the traditional industry standards of expense control by evolving or morphing them to a previously unheard of level. He disproved the notion that you can't save your way to prosperity. The company's managers and Associates are tight fisted penny pinchers who are proud of their ability to control costs. As a result, he insured Walmart's expense structure was always the lowest in the industry.

What Would Sam Do #7
BUDGET

> *"We had to keep expenses to a minimum. That is where it started. Our money was made by controlling expenses."*
>
> **Sam Walton**

ᐸᑭ *WWSD: Eight* ᑫᐳ

What Would Sam Do #8:
OVERACHIEVE

*M*r. *Sam's belief that his Associates were his business partners transformed Walmart's People Culture into one of its greatest competitive advantages.*

Above average results

Sam Walton hired hard working average people yet he set standards at above average levels. He had a unique ability to bring out the best in people. Walmart's Associates did not want to let Mr. Sam down so they would do what it took to meet or exceed his expectations. Mr. Sam turned the fierce loyalty and work ethic of his Associate partners into a powerful and insurmountable competitive advantage.

What Would Sam Do #8
OVERACHIEVE

> *"The more they know, the more they'll understand. The more they understand, the more they'll care. Once they care, there's no stopping them."*
>
> **Sam Walton**

✑ *WWSD: Nine* ✎

What Would Sam Do #9:
UNITY

M r. Sam believed it was impossible to have excellent external customer service without first having tremendous internal customer service.

Internal Service Standards

Mr. Sam's internal customer service standards reminded me of the philosophy of the Three Musketeers, 'It's all for one and one for all'! You see, Walmart not only has a high standard for external customer service but it also has a high standard for internal customer service. Sam Walton taught his

Associates to drop everything in order to help fellow Associates in need. Culturally, Sam Walton taught his team to treat one another as they would external customers.

What Would Sam Do #9
UNITY

> *"We're all working together; that's the secret."*
>
> Sam Walton

 WWSD: Ten

What Would Sam Do #10:
REINFORCE

Mr. Sam used great illustrative stories as examples to reinforce and highlight his cultural standards whenever he spoke to Walmart's managers and Associates.

Use folklore and storytelling

Sam Walton was a master storyteller who used illustrative stories to reinforce his cultural messages. Walmart's leaders continue to retell those stories to illustrate company standards in sales, customer service and expense control. Mr. Sam would often highlight a successful Associate in his stories to illustrate that every employee can make a difference. His rationale was that he knew "if one could do it, they all could do it"!

What Would Sam Do #10
REINFORCE

> *"I still can't believe it was news I get my hair cut at the barbershop. Where else would I get it cut? Why do I drive a pickup truck? What, am I supposed to haul my dogs around in a Rolls-Royce?"*
>
> **Sam Walton**

⌒ Sam Walton's ⌒
Three Basic Beliefs & Values

$\mathcal{M}$r. Sam's three basic beliefs and values remain a cultural touchstone for today's Walmart Team. Here they are presented in Walmart terms:

I. Respect for the Individual

We're hardworking, ordinary people who've teamed up to accomplish extraordinary things. While our backgrounds and personal beliefs are very different, we never take each other for granted. We encourage those around us to express their thoughts and ideas. We treat each other with dignity. This is the most basic way we show respect.

II. Service to our Customers

Our customers are the reason we're in business, so we should treat them that way. We offer quality merchandise at the lowest prices, and we do it with the best customer service possible. We look for every opportunity where we can exceed our customers' expectations. That's when we're at our very best.

III. Strive for Excellence

We're proud of our accomplishments but never satisfied. We constantly reach further to bring new ideas and goals to life. We model ourselves after Sam Walton, who was never satisfied until prices were as low as they could be or that a product's quality was as high as customers deserved and expected. We always ask: Is this the best I can do? This demonstrates the passion we have for our business, for our customers, and for our communities.

> *"We are often asked, 'What is the secret of Walmart's success?' Very simply stated, it is nothing more than the bringing together of men and women who are completely dedicated to their jobs, their company, and their communities."*
>
> **Sam Walton**
> (*From: Made in America*)

ᑲᔓ *Section Two* ᔕᐠ

WWSD #11–HONESTY:
Hire people with integrity
WWSD #12—INFORMATION:
Share the P&L
WWSD #13—LEADERSHIP:
Walk the talk
WWSD #14—PERSISTENCE:
Commit to your success
WWSD #15—EXCELLENCE:
Focus on quality not quantity
WWSD #16—BENCHMARK:
Learn from the best
WWSD #17—CLARITY:
Keep your goals focused
WWSD #18—SERVICE:
Don't forget who the boss is
WWSD #19—PARTNERSHIP:
People make the difference
WWSD #20—EDUCATE:
Teach your beliefs and values
Mr. Sam's Customer Service Commandments

 *WWSD: Eleven*

What Would Sam Do #11:
HONESTY

Mr. Sam believed he had to hire intelligent, enthusiastic people, who were honest, because he had to completely rely on them to run his stores.

Hire people with integrity

In the early days of Walmart, by necessity, Sam Walton was forced to hire people with little or no retail experience off the farms around Bentonville, Arkansas. The personal attributes he focused on when he hired were smart, energetic people, who he felt were honest. Integrity was extremely important to Mr. Sam because he had to trust his Associate business partners to serve his customers and run his stores.

What Would Sam Do #11
HONESTY

> *"You've got to give folks responsibility, you've got to trust them, and then you've got to check on them."*
>
> Sam Walton

ᑺ *WWSD: Twelve* ᑆ

What Would Sam Do #12:
INFORMATION

Mr. Sam believed the upside benefits of communicating the profit and loss statement for an individual store to the local Associates far outweighed any downside.

Share the P&L

Mr. Sam opened his books and shared the intimate details of each store's financial performance with all of his Associates. He believed each store team needed to understand the sales and expense plan to help improve their own store's performance.

Critics said the confidential information would leak to his competitors. Mr. Sam responded, "What could a competitor do to hurt Walmart even if they knew a store's actual sales & expense results?

What Would Sam Do #12
INFORMATION

> *"Information is power, and the gain you get from empowering your Associates more than offsets the risk of informing your competitor."*
>
> **Sam Walton**

෴ *WWSD: Thirteen* ෴

What Would Sam Do #13:
LEADERSHIP

When Mr. Sam visited stores he spent time personally serving customers every week of the year, so when he asked his Associates to provide great customer service they enthusiastically followed his example.

Walk the talk

Mr. Sam believed in leading by his own example by flying his own plane out to visit stores, talking with customers, and spending time with his beloved Associates every week. As servant leaders, he expected all of Walmart's managers to serve the

Associates who report to them, and to provide superior service to customers. Mr. Sam set the leadership example by modeling the behavior he expected others to follow.

What Would Sam Do #13
LEADERSHIP

> *"The real challenge for managers in a business like ours is to become what we call servant leaders. And when they do, the team – the manager and the Associates – can accomplish anything."*
>
> **Sam Walton**
> (From: *Made in America*)

ꝏ *WWSD: Fourteen* ꝏ

What Would Sam Do #14:
PERSISTENCE

Great leaders, like Sam Walton have a can-do, never say die attitude, and they have a unique ability to get those around them to buy into and share their vision, commitment, and passion.

Never give up

Whether he was born a leader or circumstances forced him to become a great leader, the cards Sam Walton was dealt in the early days of his entrepreneurial career forced him to overcome adversity. His commitment to his business, and his ability to instill a similar passion in the Associates around him, is one of the reasons Walmart survived the early challenges it faced. When the going got tough Sam Walton stayed focused on his dreams.

What Would Sam Do #14
PERSISTENCE

> *"I have always been driven to buck the system, to innovate, to take things beyond where they've been."*
>
> Sam Walton

❧ *WWSD: Fifteen* ❧

What Would Sam Do #15:
EXCELLENCE

What Sam Walton thought about 24/7/365 was making sure Walmart was the best in the world at serving its customers.

Focus on quality, not quantity

Sam Walton never wanted Walmart to be the biggest retail company in the world; he was always striving to make it the best. In his pursuit of excellence, customers clamored to his stores to take advantage of Walmart's everyday low prices. Mr. Sam stayed focused on meeting and exceeding the needs of his customers. He was rewarded handsomely as his company became the largest and most successful retailer in the world!

What Would Sam Do #15
EXCELLENCE

> *"I believe in always having goals, and always setting them high."*
>
> **Sam Walton**

WWSD: Sixteen

What Would Sam Do #16:
BENCHMARK

Mr. Sam believed that some of the best and least expensive new ideas could be found to improve Walmart by simply studying the best practices of other competitive and even non-competitive companies.

Learn from the best

Sam Walton visited the stores of his direct competitors to gather ideas he could use to improve every aspect of his store operations. Walmart also looks for ideas outside the retailing industry for ways to improve. Interestingly Walmart's leaders continue to study its small and large competitors to this day in order to find advantages which create distance between themselves and the rest of their competition!

What Would Sam Do #16
BENCHMARK

"Walmart wouldn't be what it is today without a host of fine competitors."

Sam Walton
(From: *Made in America*)

◁ *WWSD: Seventeen* ▷

What Would Sam Do #17:
CLARITY

*M*r. *Sam believed the key to success is to communicate a few clear goals and for leaders to avoid the temptation to constantly keep changing them.*

Keep your goals focused

Leaders at some companies present an ever changing set of goals to their people. If goals are constantly changing it's no wonder they aren't met. Mr. Sam was one of the best at presenting a uniform message and getting his Associates to stay focused on the same clearly defined activities. Walmart's leadership team mastered the ability to present a uniform set of strategies and tactics to the Walmart team.

What Would Sam Do #17
CLARITY

"None of our competitors has yet been able to operate on the volume that we do as efficiently as we do. They haven't been able to get their expense structure as low as ours, and they haven't been able to get their Associates to do all those extra things for their customers that ours do routinely."

Sam Walton

❦ *WWSD: Eighteen* ❦

What Would Sam Do #18:
SERVICE

*M*r. *Sam never forgot that his customers were the real boss, and they paid everyone's salary, the rent, and the utility bills!*

Don't forget who the boss is

Mr. Sam believed that the customer is your real boss if you provide products or services for purchase. The customers can choose to buy from you or they can buy from your competitor. He believed that if your customers are not treated as they expect to be treated you can bet they'll become customers of someone else who is willing to meet or exceed their expectations. Don't ever forget who your real boss is!

What Would Sam Do #18
SERVICE

> *"There is only one boss. The customer. And he can fire everybody in the company from the chairman on down, simply by spending his money somewhere else."*
>
> Sam Walton

☙ *WWSD: Nineteen* ❧

What Would Sam Do #19:
PARTNERSHIP

$\mathcal{M}$r. *Sam was so proud of Walmart's Associates that when anyone asked about Walmart's success he'd give credit where credit was due responding, "It's our people who make the difference."*

People make the difference

Sam Walton would describe his Associates as a collection of mostly average people. When asked how Walmart had achieved such incredible success, he gave all the credit to the Associates. He believed that competitors could copy his product and merchandise strategies but the one thing they could not replicate is the Walmart culture and its dedicated, enthusiastic, and loyal team of Associates.

What Would Sam Do #19
PARTNERSHIP

> *"If you take care of the people in the stores, they will take care of the customers in the same manner."*
>
> Sam Walton

ᑐᑐ *WWSD: Twenty* ᑐᑐ

What Would Sam Do #20:
EDUCATE

$\mathcal{B}$y teaching everyone his values, Sam Walton created a cultural legacy, and his personal leadership teachings remain a touchstone for Walmart's leaders even today.

Teach your beliefs/values

Sam Walton's beliefs/values are: treat the customer right, take care of your people, be honest in your dealings, pass savings along to the customer, keep things simple, think small, control costs, continuously learn, strive for excellence, and constantly improve operations. Today's Walmart leaders and Associates are still taught to embrace Mr. Sam's cultural beliefs and values.

What Would Sam Do #20
EDUCATE

> *"Each Walmart store should reflect the values of its customers and support the vision they hold for their community."*
>
> Sam Walton

✍ *Mr. Sam's* ✍
Customer Service Commandments

I.   Customers are the most important people in any business.

II.   Customers are not dependent on us; we are dependent on them.

III.   Customers are not interruptions of our work; they are the purpose of our work.

IV.   Customers do us a favor when they shop with us; we are not doing them a favor by serving them.

V.   Customers are a part of our business; they are not outsiders.

VI.   Customers are not people with whom you argue or match wits.

VII. Customers are people who bring us their wants; it is our job to fill those wants.

VIII. Customers are not cold statistics; they are flesh and blood human beings with emotions and feelings like our own.

IX. Customers are deserving of the most courteous and attentive treatment we can give them.

X. Customers are the people that make it possible to pay your salary.

XI. Customers are the lifeblood of this and every other business.

"Our time-proven philosophy of offering our customers the best value in town, good quality at the lowest price, is even more appealing in this changing marketplace. Our plan is to make our stores continuing testimonials to the sign on the front of every store: 'We Sell for Less'."

Sam Walton

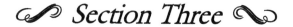

Section Three

WWSD #21–INFLUENCE:
Provide inspired leadership

WWSD #22–OPPORTUNITY
Take risks and be innovative

WWSD #23–INNOVATION
Embrace change like a friend

WWSD #24–GUARANTEE
Stand behind your products

WWSD #25–COMPETITION
Compete to win

WWSD #26–LISTENING
Get close to your customers

WWSD #27–IMPROVEMENT
Keep getting better

WWSD #28–THINK SMALL
Reduce complexity

WWSD #29–VISION
Challenge the status quo

WWSD #30–COMMITMENT
Require people to commit

Mr. Sam's 11 Key Walmart Leadership Competencies

ᦉ *WWSD: Twenty-One* ᦉ

What Would Sam Do #21:
INFLUENCE

Visionary, transformational
leaders like Sam Walton are few and far
between, but when they surface, they achieve
remarkable things.

Provide inspired leadership

Sam Walton was a down to earth leader who brought out the best in others. He achieved success with people because he was a servant leader who led by his own example. He never asked anyone to do anything he hadn't already proven he was willing to do. He believed people don't need to be managed they need to be lead by caring leaders. Posthumously, around the world, Sam Walton remains Walmart's charismatic leadership icon.

What Would Sam Do #21
INFLUENCE

> *"I like to set goals and budgets and have done so all these many years. Usually we have exceeded even my most optimistic goals due to our great people and their attitudes towards satisfying our customers."*
>
> Sam Walton

ᕦ WWSD: Twenty-Two ᕤ

What Would Sam Do #22:
OPPORTUNITY

The leaders at Walmart were always willing to take risks and make mistakes because they always knew that Mr. Sam would support them.

Take risks and be innovative

Sam Walton was an innovator who shunned conventional wisdom in favor of blazing his own trails. He believed that if everybody else was doing it *this* way, he'd try doing it *that* way. He encouraged people to take risks and try new approaches and new ideas. Most organizations say they value risk-taking, but then they fire people who fail; not Sam Walton!

What Would Sam Do #22
OPPORTUNITY

> *"I guess in all my years, what I heard more often than anything was a town of less than 50,000 population cannot support a discount store for very long."*
>
> Sam Walton

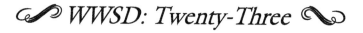 *WWSD: Twenty-Three*

What Would Sam Do #23:
INNOVATION

*M*r. *Sam encouraged everyone who worked at Walmart to look at every policy, procedure and practice and he expected them to recommend changes that would improve every area of the store or distribution center operation.*

Embrace change like a friend

Sam Walton was an initiator and instigator of change, and for this reason, Walmart became a fast adapter to changes in the marketplace. If something works Walmart sticks with it and continuously works to improve it. If something isn't working they change it, fix it, or discard it.

Change is the norm at Walmart and its managers and Associates, just like Sam Walton, embrace change like a welcomed friend.

What Would Sam Do #23
INNOVATION

> *"Keep everybody guessing as to what your next trick is going to be,"* he said. *"Don't become too predictable."*
>
> Sam Walton

ᏅᎧ *WWSD: Twenty-Four* ᏅᎧ

What Would Sam Do #24:
GUARANTEE

Mr. Sam would accept merchandise returns for good reasons, bad reasons or no reason whatsoever; he even knowingly accepted product returns for products which were never even carried in his stores.

Stand behind your products

Mr. Sam put his service desk at the very front of the Walmart Store where all of his customers, who were checking out, could observe the customers who were returning merchandise. At Walmart the customer is always right and Sam Walton wanted everyone to see how customers with a merchandise problem were treated. His *satisfaction 100% guaranteed* policy is one of the ways he built customer loyalty.

What Would Sam Do #24
GUARANTEE

> *"The two most important words I ever wrote were on that first Walmart sign: 'Satisfaction Guaranteed' . . . they have made all the difference."*
>
> Sam Walton

ᑲᔆᕽ WWSD: Twenty-Five ᕽᑭᐧ

What Would Sam Do #25:
COMPETITION

*S*am Walton taught his Walmart team to enjoy the spirit of competition, and not surprisingly, Mr. Sam actually always seemed to enjoy the competition more than the ultimate victory.

Compete to win

From Sam Walton's perspective, survival of the fittest was the natural order of things. As an athlete, who relished competing and winning, Mr. Sam enjoyed the competition as much as the ultimate victory. In business, he would do whatever it took to develop a strategy to beat his competition. He believed in studying his competition and then he'd out-think, out-work and out-execute his competitor in order to win.

What Would Sam Do #25
COMPETITION

> *"Our people want to win so badly that they just go out there and do it. Even though everybody has told them they can't succeed, they just go out there and succeed anyway."*
>
> Sam Walton

ᏯᏨ *WWSD: Twenty-Six* ᏨᏮ

What Would Sam Do #26:
LISTENING

The Walmart brand is respected around the world, and I think that's because Mr. Sam understood the importance of listening to his customers.

Get close to your customers

Sam Walton used an outside-in approach to decide the kinds of products and services to offer his customers. By asking his current customers for new product ideas he was able to focus in a laser-like fashion on their wants and needs. As large as Walmart has become its buyers and store managers still have the ability to provide products that cater to the needs of local customers in cities around the world.

What Would Sam Do #26
LISTENING

> *"The key to success is to get out into the store and listen to what the Associates have to say. It's terribly important for everyone to get involved. Our best ideas come from clerks and stock personnel."*
>
> Sam Walton

ல் WWSD: Twenty-Seven ல்

What Would Sam Do #27:
IMPROVEMENT

Mr. Sam valued and practiced continuous improvement and learning long before the total quality experts began teaching them.

Keep getting better

Sam Walton believed that individuals and teams are either improving their performance in every area or they are going backwards and getting worse. Maintaining the status quo isn't an option at Walmart. Mr. Sam believed you can't simply maintain the status quo and expect to be a market leader. He knew that if he failed to innovate and improve that his aggressive competitors would steal his competitive advantage in the marketplace.

What Would Sam Do #27
IMPROVEMENT

> *"I had to pick myself up and get on with it, do it all over again, only even better this time."*
>
> Sam Walton

☙ WWSD: Twenty-Eight ❧

What Would Sam Do #28:
THINK SMALL

*S*am Walton's most successful *strategies are easy to understand in concept, but they require tremendous discipline for others to implement.*

Reduce Complexity

Many leaders were taught, and teach others, to overly complicate their strategies. They learned to "think big, start small and scale up". Sam Walton simplified his business with the strategy, "think small, start small and scale up". Mr. Sam knew that complex strategies are destined to fail at the point of execution. By simplifying everything they do, Walmart's leaders are able to implement strategies that have a better chance of succeeding.

What Would Sam Do #28
THINK SMALL

> *"Our most famous technique for doing this is a textbook example of thinking small. We call it 'Store within a Store', and it is the simplest idea in the world."*
>
> **Sam Walton**
> (From: *Made in America*)

ᐸᶨ *WWSD: Twenty-Nine* ᶩᐳ

What Would Sam Do #29:
VISION

*M*r. *Sam made certain change is a way of life at Walmart; he knew the competitive world is constantly changing, and he could not simply maintain the status quo, and still expect to be a market leader.*

Challenge the status quo

Sam Walton once said that there wasn't a day throughout his adult life that he didn't think about how he could improve some aspect of his business. He constantly thought about new products, services, and how to improve customer service. With his legal pad close at hand he'd capture his ideas on paper. Once Mr. Sam came up with a good idea he'd develop the new concept and then he'd try to implement it immediately.

What Would Sam Do #29
VISION

> *"Capital isn't scarce; vision is."*
>
> Sam Walton

 WWSD: Thirty

What Would Sam Do #30:
COMMITMENT

Sam Walton expected people to not only work hard but he also expected his team to achieve the company's aggressive goals each day.

Require people to commit

Sam Walton expected people who worked at Walmart to give 100% every day. Because of his high standards for remaining in-stock, and for moving customers through the check-out lines with minimal delay, his employees were required to work extremely hard every hour of the work day. It takes a high level of commitment and a strong work ethic to work for Walmart; anything less was unacceptable to Sam Walton.

What Would Sam Do #30
COMMITMENT

"Commit to your business. Believe in it more than anybody else."

Sam Walton
(From: *Made in America*)

❧ Mr. Sam's 11 Key ☙ Walmart Leadership Competencies

Five People Skills

1. <u>Communication</u>—The role of managers is to give Associates the help, information, and motivation needed to serve the customers.

2. <u>Developing Others</u>—The ability to develop the talents and potential of every Associate must be the goal of every manager.

3. <u>Motivating Others</u>—A manager's true success is measured by his or her ability to help others be more successful.

4. <u>Customer Focus</u>—Associates at every level must be empowered to respond to the needs of customers.

5. <u>Listening</u>—Leaders at all levels are expected to spend time with Associates

listening to and responding to their concerns.

Six Work Processes

1. Continuous Improvement—Any process, policy, or practice can potentially be improved and everyone is encouraged to take a critical look at ways to improve the business.

2. Sense of Urgency—"Do it now" accurately describes the company's bias for action.

3. Team Development—A manager's primary responsibility is to serve the Associates he or she leads. Walmart believes in the spirit of teamwork and the synergy it creates.

4. Organization/Planning—At Walmart being organized and having a good plan in place can be the difference between being completely overwhelmed versus thriving in an often chaotic environment.

5. Expectations/Accountability—High expectations are the key to everything and operational excellence is the standard everyone tries to achieve.

6. <u>Resolving Problems</u>—The retail work environment presents an endless number of problem resolution opportunities. People who succeed at Walmart enjoy addressing a wide array of problems.

> *"From the time our customers enter a Walmart Store until the time they leave our Associates endeavor to provide the warmest, most friendly, most helpful, and most appreciative environment in which to shop."*
>
> **Sam Walton**

Section Four

WWSD #31–IMITATION:

Research your competition

WWSD #32–CUSTOMER-CENTERED

Look out for customers

WWSD #33–PERSEVERENCE

Never become complacent

WWSD #34–ANALYZE

One customer at a time

WWSD #35–EXECUTION

Execute, execute, execute

WWSD #36–PROACTIVE

Be decisive

WWSD #37–RISKTAKING

Take managed risks

WWSD #38–EXPECTATIONS

Set aggressive standards

WWSD #39–TACTICS

Manageable strategies

WWSD #40–STUDY

Learn from other's success

Sam Walton's 10 Rules for Success

ᒼᕞ *WWSD: Thirty-One* ᕞᒼ

What Would Sam Do #31:
IMITATION

S*am Walton required his managers and buyers to visit his competitor's stores each week to seek out and find new ideas Walmart could replicate quickly in its own stores!*

Research your competition

Mr. Sam visited his competitor's stores to find out what they were doing right; he could have cared less what they were doing wrong. By shopping in their stores, he learned their merchandising, product, and service secrets and his competitors learned Walmart's strategies and tactics in the same way. He believed in "borrowing ideas shamelessly" from others, especially because they were free and plentiful.

What Would Sam Do #31
IMITATION

> *"We at Walmart are just absolute fanatics about our managers and buyers getting off their chairs and getting out into those stores. We've drummed into their heads they should come back with at least one idea that will pay for the trip."*
>
> **Sam Walton**
> (From: *Made in America*)

⚜ *WWSD: Thirty-Two* ⚜

What Would Sam Do #32:
CUSTOMER FOCUSED

S*am Walton taught his company* buyers to negotiate the lowest possible prices with manufacturers and suppliers on behalf of Walmart's customers.

Look out for customers

Mr. Sam generated his profits by selling high volumes of products at the lowest possible prices; that's what discount retailing is all about. By buying in large quantities he was able to purchase at the lowest possible prices and then he'd pass the savings along to his customers. His goal was to offer too good to be true bargains to the legions of loyal Walmart shoppers, so they'd return to shop again and again.

What Would Sam Do #32
CUSTOMER FOCUSED

> *"They want clean, neat stores that are in-stock and merchandised with low prices and high quality."*
>
> Sam Walton

⚜ *WWSD: Thirty-Three* ⚜

What Would Sam Do #33:
PERSEVERANCE

Sam Walton made certain no one on his leadership team ever became complacent because he knew that companies that aren't willing to adapt and change are destined to fail.

Never become complacent

No matter how successful Walmart had become, Sam Walton was never satisfied with maintaining the status quo. He feared success might make his Walmart team complacent. Obsessively, Mr. Sam maintained his competitive vigilance, so his team could always stay at least one step ahead of his competitors. He knew from his own early business experiences that past success was no guarantee of future success.

What Would Sam Do #33
PERSEVERANCE

> *"I think I overcame every single one of my personal shortcomings by the sheer passion I brought to my work. I don't know if you're born with this kind of passion, or if you can learn it. But I do know you need it."*
>
> **Sam Walton**

ᐱ *WWSD: Thirty-Four* ᐱ

What Would Sam Do #34:
ANALYZE

*M*r. *Sam believed the key to solving chain-wide problems in a large retail company like Walmart was to figure out how to design a solution for a single store.*

One customer at a time

Whenever Walmart leaders need to make a big decision impacting thousands of stores they use a simplification lesson taught by Mr. Sam. He told them to think in terms of one store at a time, one department at a time, and one customer at a time. By doing this, Walmart's leaders would prove to themselves whether an idea was viable at a single store before they would try to implement it in a large number of stores across the country.

What Would Sam Do #34
ANALYZE

> *"When we sit down to talk about our business, we like to spend time focusing on a single store, and how that store is doing against a single competitor in that particular market."*
>
> **Sam Walton**

WWSD: Thirty-Five

What Would Sam Do #35:
EXECUTION

Mr. Sam always wanted Walmart to execute strategies as if it were a small company because he knew that most organizations become much less flexible as they become larger.

Execute, execute, execute

Changing directions at most large companies is like trying to turn an aircraft carrier. Walmart, on the other hand, has remained nimble, changing directions like a PT boat. Mr. Sam didn't have to "negotiate" course changes with company leaders because his team was trained to execute directives. While some of his competitors had difficulty implementing new ideas, Walmart's team implemented its strategies with lockstep execution.

What Would Sam Do #35
EXECUTION

> *"Our folks don't expect something for nothing, and they don't expect things to come easily. Our method of success, as I see it, is ACTION, with a capital 'A' and a lot of hard work."*
>
> **Sam Walton**

ᴄᴈᴘ *WWSD: Thirty-Six* ᴈᴏ

What Would Sam Do #36:
PROACTIVE

*M*r. *Sam realized when he designed a strategy that ninety percent of any strategy is the tactical execution of it.*

Be decisive

When faced with a new challenge Sam Walton would always err on the side of action rather than inaction. He believed in quickly establishing a game plan and then decisively executing against that plan. He knew he'd make mistakes along the way so he was always willing to adjust his strategy to match the changes in the competitive environment. Mr. Sam was not afraid to make tough decisions and he enjoyed taking managed risks.

What Would Sam Do #36
PROACTIVE

"There are a lot of people out there who have some great ideas, but nothing in the world is cheaper that than a good idea without action behind it. The problem usually is finding someone who is willing to implement it."

Sam Walton

WWSD: Thirty-Seven

What Would Sam Do #37:
RISKTAKING

S*am Walton believed if his competitors were all doing something one way, he'd try doing it in a different, opposite or unconventional way always in search of an advantage.*

Take managed risks

When he first started Walmart, Sam Walton admitted he failed nine out of ten times in those early days, when he took risks. He believed it was that one time out of ten when he succeeded, that made all of those failures worthwhile! Walmart leaders encourage risk-taking, knowing if something doesn't work, they'll make adjustments and try something else. Mr. Sam knew that only by taking managed risks can you find the competitive advantage.

What Would Sam Do #37
RISKTAKING

"Ignore the conventional wisdom. If everybody else is doing it one way, there's a good chance you can find your niche by going in exactly the opposite direction."

Sam Walton

ᒉᗡ *WWSD: Thirty-Eight* ᗡᒉ

What Would Sam Do #38:
EXPECTATIONS

*S*am Walton knew if he wanted *Walmart to be the best at serving customers he had to get his team to help set, and achieve, very aggressive goals.*

Set aggressive standards

The key to operational excellence at Walmart is the creation and achievement of its aggressive goals that require stretch to reach. Mr. Sam used an acronym, "H.E.A.T.K.T.E." to focus company leaders and each Associate on reaching the highest standards. HEATKTE stands for, "High

Expectations Are The Key To Everything."
When leaders set the bar high people will
feel challenged to work to achieve even the
loftiest goals.

What Would Sam Do #38
EXPECTATIONS

> *"We need to constantly keep in mind that exceeding our customer's expectations is our number one priority."*
>
> Sam Walton

ᑫᔑ *WWSD: Thirty-Nine* ᕲᔓ

What Would Sam Do #39:
TACTICS

*M*r. Sam believed it was imperative for company leaders to design clear strategies that were simple enough for others to actually implement in Walmart's stores.

Manageable strategies

At Walmart, if you couldn't explain an idea, concept or strategy in simple terms, on a single page of paper, Sam Walton believed it was too complicated to implement out in Walmart's stores. Because of his experience working in his stores, he understood the importance of designing solutions that were easy to implement. Mr. Sam knew that ideas are the easy part; it's the implementation of those great ideas that often proves difficult.

What Would Sam Do #39
TACTICS

> *"We've said it through the year—do it, try it, fix it. Not a bad approach—and it works."*
>
> **Sam Walton**

ᐂ *WWSD: Forty* ᐁ

What Would Sam Do #40:
STUDY

*M*r. *Sam looked inside and outside the retail industry for great low cost ideas he could copy and imitate in Walmart's stores.*

Learn from other's success

As a continuous learner, Mr. Sam was always trying to learn a better way of doing things from everyone around him. He often met with leaders from other companies to share ideas and learn their company's best practices. When he discovered a great new idea he'd quickly go to work trying to figure out how to implement it at Walmart. Mr. Sam liked to imitate the proven strategies because the cost of copying them was usually low.

What Would Sam Do #40
STUDY

> *"We tried to make up for our lack of experience and sophistication by spending as much time as we could checking-out the competition."*
>
> **Sam Walton**
> (From: *Made in America*)

❧ *Mr. Sam's* ❧
10 Rules for Success

1. **Commit to your business.** Believe in it more than anything else. If you love your work, you'll be out there every day trying to do the best you can, and pretty soon everybody around will catch the passion from you—like a fever.

2. **Share your profits with all your Associates, and treat them as partners.** In turn, they will treat you as a partner, and together you will all perform beyond your wildest expectations.

3. **Motivate your partners.** Money and ownership aren't enough. Set high goals, encourage competition and

then keep score. Make bets with outrageous payoffs.

4. **Communicate everything you possibly can to your partners.** The more they know, the more they'll understand. The more they understand, the more they'll care. Once they care, there's no stopping them. Information is power, and the gain you get from empowering your Associates more than offsets the risk of informing your competitors.

5. **Appreciate everything your Associates do for the business.** Nothing else can quite substitute for a few well-chosen, well-timed, sincere words of praise. They're absolutely free and worth a fortune.

6. **Celebrate your success and find humor in your failures.** Don't take yourself so seriously. Loosen up and everyone around you will loosen up. Have fun and always show

enthusiasm. When all else fails put on a costume and sing a silly song.

7. **Listen to everyone in your company, and figure out ways to get them talking.** The folks on the front line—the ones who actually talk to customers—are the only ones who really know what's going on out there. You'd better find out what they know.

8. **Exceed your customer's expectations.** If you do they'll come back over and over. Give them what they want—and a little more. Let them know you appreciate them. Make good on all your mistakes, and don't make excuses—apologize. Stand behind everything you do. 'Satisfaction guaranteed' will make all the difference.

9. **Control your expenses better than your competition.** This is where you can always find the competitive advantage. You can make a lot of mistakes and still recover if you run an efficient operation.

Or you can be brilliant and still go out of business if you're too inefficient.

10. **Swim upstream.** Go the other way. Ignore the conventional wisdom. If everybody is doing it one way, there's a good chance you can find your niche by going exactly in the opposite direction.

From: *Made in America, My Story;* by Sam Walton; published by Doubleday.

> *"Our years of success and profitable growth are a direct result of our Associate's innovative ideas, commitment, suggestions, entrepreneurial spirit, and hard work."*
>
> **Sam Walton**

 *Section Five*

WWSD #41—SYNERGY:
Achieve team goals

WWSD #42—CELEBRATION
Have fun as you work

WWSD #43—CHANGE
Continuous improvement

WWSD #44—BELIEVE
Have faith in people

WWSD #45—URGENCY
Don't wait to do it later

WWSD #46—COLLECT
Ask people for ideas

WWSD #47—LOYALTY
Exceed customer expectations

WWSD #48—TEAMWORK
Value team players

WWSD #49—EFFORT
Outwork your competition

WWSD #50—APPRECIATION
Give credit to others

Mr. Sam's Glossary of Walmart Terminology
Sam Walton Biography
Timeline of Events in Sam Walton's Life
About the Author—Michael Bergdahl

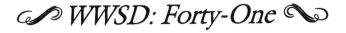 WWSD: Forty-One

What Would Sam Do #41:
SYNERGY

Sam Walton's ability to get company leaders to forgo their own self-serving, egotistical needs, in favor of team goals is one of the great success stories of the Walmart culture.

Achieve team goals

Sam Walton's ability to leverage the synergy created by teams of people is one of the towering strengths of Walmart's culture. Servant leadership is the foundation and the secret behind Sam Walton's ability to achieve team synergy. By using Golden

Rule principles the company's team leaders prove to the Associates they care about them, which creates trust, strong teams, and ultimately team synergy.

What Would Sam Do #41
SYNERGY

"It is amazing what a team of people can accomplish if no one worries about who will get the credit in the end."

Sam Walton

☙ WWSD: Forty-Two ❧

What Would Sam Do #42:
CELEBRATION

S*am Walton truly believed that employees with good attitudes have a positive effect on customer attitudes, which in turn positively impacts business performance.*

Have fun as you work

Sam Walton encouraged people to have fun at work. Managers are encouraged to create unusual contests to keep people motivated. The winning team might get to publicly dunk the opposing team's manager in a dunking booth or the losing manager

123

might shave his head or wear a wacky costume around the store! Regardless of the approach Sam Walton knew happy employees yield happy customers.

What Would Sam Do #42
CELEBRATION

> *"Celebrate your successes. Find some humor in your failures. Don't take yourself so seriously. Loosen up, and everybody around you will loosen up. Have fun. Show enthusiasm—always."*
>
> **Sam Walton**

↶ WWSD: Forty-Three ↷

What Would Sam Do #43:
CHANGE

Sam Walton realized that finding a small improvement in one store represented big improvement in terms of dollars when taken and implemented across the entire chain of Walmart stores.

Continuous improvement

If it ain't broke, break it aptly describes Sam Walton's philosophy on continuously improving his business. He believed in the Japanese concept "kaizen" meaning small improvements each day would eventually lead to big improvements in the long run. He was even interested in improvement ideas that only saved a few dollars. Mr. Sam believed every area at Walmart could be improved; there were no sacred cows!

What Would Sam Do #43
CHANGE

> *"I've made it my own personal mission to ensure that constant change is a vital part of the Walmart culture itself. I've forced change— sometimes for change's sake alone – at every turn in the company's development."*
>
> Sam Walton

 *WWSD: Forty-Four*

What Would Sam Do #44:
BELIEVE

Walmart hires mostly average people, trains them to do things 'The Walmart Way' and then promotes many of them quickly, often before they are ready, into positions of greater responsibility.

Have faith in people

In the early days, Mr. Sam hired people off the farms around his home office in Bentonville even though most had no retailing experience. He knew he could teach people the skills needed if they had a good attitude and were willing to work hard.

Often, Sam Walton believed in people more than they believed in their own abilities. His confidence in them gave people the belief that they would succeed and the vast majority of them did!

What Would Sam Do #44
BELIEVE

> *"Outstanding leaders go out of their way to boost the self-esteem of their personnel. If people believe in themselves, it's amazing what they can accomplish. Desire and a willingness to work make up for a lack of experience."*
>
> **Sam Walton**

 *WWSD: Forty-Five*

What Would Sam Do #45:
URGENCY

Sam Walton believed hard work, long hours, and enjoying the pressure of hitting deadlines are the key ingredients an individual must have to achieve success in business and in life.

Don't wait to do it later

Sam Walton modeled his cultural standards for getting things done, NOW! He even created a company rule, a version of the old adage, "don't put off until tomorrow what you can do today." His "sundown rule" requires the company's managers and

Associates to follow-up on requests, take or return phone calls, and respond to e-mail requests before the work day ends; only then can they go home.

What Would Sam Do #45
URGENCY

> *"What we guard against around here is people saying, 'Let's think about it.' We make a decision. Then we act on it."*
>
> Sam Walton

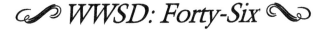

WWSD: Forty-Six

What Would Sam Do #46:
COLLECT

Sam Walton knew he hadn't cornered the market on good ideas and that's why he was constantly reaching out to learn from the experiences of others.

Ask people for ideas

The people closest to the work almost always have the best solutions to an organization's problems. It is for this reason Sam Walton openly solicited ideas and input from his own Associates. The "people greeter" in Walmart's stores is an excellent example of a good idea in one store being implemented across all of Walmart's stores. Mr. Sam collected good ideas from his team and then he implemented the best ideas in his stores.

What Would Sam Do #46
COLLECT

"I probably have traveled and walked into more stores than anybody in America. I am just trying to get ideas, any kind of ideas that will help our company. Most of us don't invent ideas. We take the best ideas from someone else."

Sam Walton

ভ *WWSD: Forty-Seven* ও

What Would Sam Do #47:
LOYALTY

M̲r. Sam figured out that when you make your customers your number one priority, they show their appreciation by bringing you their business over and over again.

Exceed customer expectations

Mr. Sam challenged his Associates to practice, "aggressive hospitality." The goal was to get all of his Associates to approach customers, smile, greet them, and offer assistance. Sam Walton believed the key to Walmart's success was to give service above and beyond what customers ordinarily expect. In response his customers would reward his company by returning and spending their money every week of the year.

What Would Sam Do #47
LOYALTY

> *"Our customers tell us they like you, individually and collectively. They like your friendly helpful attitude, they know you want to help them and treat them personally with respect. In other words, your service and dedication come through loud and clear."*

Sam Walton

ᚙ *WWSD: Forty-Eight* ᚙ

What Would Sam Do #48:
TEAMWORK

*M*r. *Sam believed you can't just call a group of individuals working in proximity to one another a team, and assume as a leader you are gaining the synergies and benefits of real teamwork.*

Value team players

Sam Walton valued team success more highly at Walmart than individual success. That's because he believed that individuals don't win in business but teams do. For this reason, egotistical, recognition seeking prima donna's don't do well at

Walmart. Team players, who are willing to share their success with others, are highly valued and rewarded. Associates often say their store team is so close it's like being part of a "Walmart family."

What Would Sam Do #48
TEAMWORK

> *"Individuals don't win. Teams do."*
>
> **Sam Walton**

∾ *WWSD: Forty-Nine* ∾

What Would Sam Do #49:
EFFORT

Sam Walton spent his every waking moment trying to improve Walmart. He did it by out-thinking, out-working, and out-executing his competition.

Outwork your competition

Mr. Sam had a legendary work ethic. He was known for arriving at work at 3:00 or 4:00 in the morning, often 7 days each week. He required all of the company's managers, at the home office, to work on Saturdays. Sam Walton felt it was important for the leaders of the company to set the example for the rest of the Associates. While K-Mart's leaders were having a day off on Saturday, Walmart's leaders were at work plotting strategies against them!

What Would Sam Do #49
EFFORT

"I always had confidence that as long as we did our work and were good to our customers there would be no limit to us."

Sam Walton

⧼ WWSD: Fifty ⧽

What Would Sam Do #50:
APPRECIATION

Mr. Sam believed from the bottom of his heart that Walmart's Associates, his army of employees, were the key to the success of his company.

Give credit to others

In his mind, Sam Walton flipped the organizational pyramid at Walmart placing the employees who provided service to the customers at the top and everyone else in the organization beneath them. When visiting stores he always spent time speaking one on one with his beloved Associates. Mr. Sam told the corporate staff he considered the Associates in contact with the customers in the stores the most important people in the company.

What Would Sam Do #50
APPRECIATION

> *"Appreciate everything your Associates do for the business. Nothing else can quite substitute for a few well-chosen, well-timed, sincere words of praise. They're absolutely free and worth a fortune."*
>
> Sam Walton

◡❧ *Mr. Sam's* ❧◡
Glossary of Walmart Terminology

Aggressive Hospitality—Approach customers, smile, say hello, and ask if you can help the customer find what they are looking for. If a customer asks for help finding a product, Walmart's Associates are expected to stop what they are doing and take the customer to the shelf where the desired product is located.

Associate—Mr. Sam's term for a Walmart "employee".

Associate Opinion Survey—A Survey given to Walmart's Associates periodically designed to give every single Associate a formalized way to voice their ideas, suggestions, and concerns.

Associate Partnership—Mr. Sam believed in treating his '"employees" as business partners.

Boss Concept—The customer is the boss and can fire everyone at Walmart from the chairman on down by simply deciding to spend their money elsewhere.

Diversity—Each Associate brings different experience, ideas, and know-how to Walmart and it is from this diversity the company draws its strength.

Embracing Change—Mr. Sam believed change is a way of life at Walmart and he expected everyone to embrace change like a welcomed friend.

Empowerment—Push decision making downward giving local store managers and Associates the responsibility and authority needed to provide superior customer service.

EDLP—Mr. Sam made sure his products were ALWAYS sold at Every Day Low Prices to insure his customers could save money and live better.

Exceed our Customer's Expectations— Provide customer service that isn't just good . . . but legendary.

Expense Control—Managers and Associates are expected to manage company expenses in a thrifty manner, in the same way they would if they themselves were writing a personal check to pay for them.

Goal Setting—Set goals high enough so that you always have to stretch to reach them.

Golden Rule—Mr. Sam's believed that everyone deserves to be treated with the respect and dignity. Treat others the way you would want to be treated.

Grass Roots Process—Mr. Sam coached every Walmart manager to listen to the Associates because he found in his own experience the Associates are the single best generators of new ideas. Periodically, a more formalized grass roots process is utilized at Walmart to gather Associate input called the "Associate Opinion Survey". The survey is designed to give every single Associate a way to voice their ideas, suggestions, and concerns. Using the Grass Roots Process and the Associate Opinion Survey Mr. Sam credited all of Walmart's Associates for making Walmart one of the most admired companies in the world!

HEATKTE—HIGH EXPECTATIONS ARE THE KEY TO EVERYTHING.

Hire for Attitude—Hire people who have a good attitude and then teach them "The

Walmart Way" and the skills they will need to succeed.

Internal Customer Service—Mr. Sam expected everyone on the Walmart team to drop everything they were doing to help their fellow Associates whenever support was requested.

Integrity—Mr. Sam would go a long way to help his managers or Associates who were having job performance problems but he wouldn't take the first step with someone who had proven to him that they lacked integrity.

Lagniappe—Giving the customer something a little extra that they didn't expect but Walmart knows they are sure to like.

MBWA—Mr. Sam believed in management by wandering around. He felt every manager needs to get out of their office and go out and spend quality time talking with Associates and customers.

Merchandising Excellence—Having the right products, at the right place, at the right time, and at the right price.

New Ideas—Mr. Sam believed the best new ideas could be found by asking and then listening to the company's managers and Associates, or by asking suppliers or even customers for input.

One Stop Shopping—Mr. Sam's goal was to offer a wide array of products and services so that customers could find whatever they needed under one roof at their local Walmart Store.

Open Door—If any Associate had a problem they needed to discuss with a manager Mr. Sam personally guaranteed his management team would have "an open door as well as an open mind" to insure Associate concerns were dealt with fairly.

Ownership—The belief that all of Walmart's Associates are business partners, and so many own company stock that Sam Walton believed they should act like business owners. Mr. Sam would say, *If someone asks you who owns Walmart tell them that you do!*

People "Our people make the difference" —Sam Walton was dedicated to a philosophy that continuing controlled, profitable growth can only be managed by people, not programs, not systems, but the right people—Walmart people.

People Greeter—Mr. Sam believed that having a people greeter was a sincere and friendly way to personally welcome Walmart's friends and neighbors as they entered their local Walmart store.

Respect—Respect for customers, respect for Associates, respect for suppliers, and respect for one another is at the core of all of Walmart's rules, customs, and its culture. Mr. Sam believed being respectful is not only the key to building relationships with people; it is also the key to building a business committed to excellence.

Satisfaction 100% Guaranteed—Mr. Sam was the first to put his service desk at the front of the store so all of the customers who were in the checkout lines could clearly see how those with problems were handled.

Servant Leadership—First Associates need to know their managers care about them, second managers need to lead by their own example using Golden Rule Values, and third managers need to spend time supporting those Associates who report to them.

Shared Agenda—Everyone at Walmart regardless of job is expected to share one common agenda which focuses on "The Customer."

Store within a Store—Everyone on the Walmart team at the local store level needs to "think small" as if they work for a single retail store rather than a massive retail chain. The focus needs to be on one store at a time, one department at a time, and one customer at a time. Department managers are encouraged to run their departments as if they were entrepreneurs in their own business.

Sundown Rule—Don't put off until tomorrow what you can do today.

Teamwork—Teams win, not individuals. The goal of teams and teamwork is ultimately to achieve team synergy. To Mr. Sam that meant the accomplishments of an effective team are greater than the sum of the contributions of the individual team members. In other words, to achieve team synergy, "the whole must always be greater than the sum of the parts."

Ten Foot Rule—When a customer comes within ten feet of an Associate that Associate needs "drop everything they are doing' and focus on serving the customer.

The Walmart Way—A phrase often used to summarize Walmart's unconventional approach to business. The fact is Walmart has its own unique way of doing things with an unrelenting focus on quality, customer service, excellence, productivity, expense management, continuous improvement, and valuing diversity. The Sam Walton way IS The Walmart Way.

Three Beliefs and Values—1. Respect for the Individual; 2. Service to our Customers; 3. Strive for Excellence.

Two Rules of Customer Service—Rule #1: the customer is always right . . . Rule #2: when the customer is wrong refer to Rule #1.

Vendor Partnership—Mr. Sam's unique relationship with his vendor partners was built on trust, based on the assumption of total integrity, allowing full disclosure and sharing of confidential product sales information.

Walmart Cheer—It's a fun way to make sure every Associate feels part of the Walmart family, and at the same time, it is a way to maintain the focus on providing great customer service.

Yes We Can Sam—A program for gathering money saving ideas from all Associates. If Mr. Sam found an Associate had a great cost saving idea at one store he would quickly take steps to implement that same idea across all of Walmart's stores. The net result of taking even a small cost saving idea at one store, and implementing it across the entire chain, was a big cost saving overall.

ᑫᔐ *Sam Walton Biography* ᑫᔐ

> ## "I always wanted Walmart to be the best retailer in the world, not necessarily the biggest."
>
> ### Sam Walton

Samuel Moore "Sam" Walton was the founder of Wal-Mart Stores and Sam's Club, the world's largest retailer and the world's largest company. Today, the annual sales of Walmart are on track to soon reach half a trillion dollars.

Sam Walton was born on March 29, 1918 in Kingfisher, Oklahoma. In the early 1920's, his family moved to Missouri where he became the youngest Eagle Scout in that state's history. He was an excellent athlete who excelled at basketball and football in high school. As the team's quarterback, for Columbia, Missouri's Hickman High School, his team won the state football championship.

Growing up during the Great Depression meant he had to do whatever he could to help his family financially, including milking cows, and delivering milk, along with newspapers, to people in their neighborhood.

After graduating from high school Sam Walton studied at the University of Missouri-Columbia where he earned a degree in Economics. On campus he was an officer in the ROTC, senior class president, and a member of several prestigious fraternities including the Zeta Phi chapter of Beta Theta Pi fraternity, and the professional business fraternity, Alpha Kappa Psi.

He served as a captain in Army Intelligence during World War II. It was around that same time he met Helen Robson, to whom he was married for close to 50 years. Following the war he decided to open his own retail store. His father-in-law loaned him the initial $20,000 to help him open his first Ben Franklin variety store, in Arkansas. Sam's low price strategies allowed him to drive high volume sales which in turn allowed him to negotiate lower prices with his wholesalers. Forced to close his store in Newport, due to a lease he was unable to renew, Sam Walton decided to open his own store in Bentonville, Arkansas called *Walton's Five and Dime.*

In 1962, he opened his first *Wal-Mart Discount City* in Rogers, Arkansas. He transferred his low price products philosophy from his Ben Franklin stores to his own Wal-Mart stores in the process. His simple goal was "to raise the standard of living for people living in rural America to match the standard of living of people living in urban areas." The company he founded 50 years ago now has more than 10,000 stores worldwide.

Here are just some of Sam Walton and Walmart's achievements. Walmart was named *Retailer of the 20th Century* by Discount Store News and it made the list of *100 Best Companies To Work For*. It was ranked on Financial Times' *Most Respected in the World* list. In 2011 Walmart was named *Top Corporation for Diversity* by Diversity Business.com. In 2002, based on its annual sales, Walmart became the number one company on the FORTUNE 500 List. In 2003, and again in 2004, Walmart was named FORTUNE Magazine's *Most Admired Company in the USA*. FORBES Magazine recognized Walmart Stores as the *Number One Most Generous Company*, making US$913 million in charitable contributions from Walmart, its Foundation, its customers and its Associates around the globe in its fiscal year ending 2011.

Sam Walton received the *Presidential Medal of Freedom* from George H. W. Bush in 1992. By the end of his life, Sam Walton had amassed a US$100 billion personal fortune, which made him the world's richest man. Sam Walton died of bone cancer on April 5, 1992.

 *Sam Walton Timeline*

1918   Born March 29, in Kingfisher, Oklahoma.

1936   Graduated from Hickman High School in Missouri.

1940   University of Missouri Graduation, B.A. in Economics.

1942-45 Served as a Captain in U.S. Army Intelligence.

1943   Married his wife Helen, they had 4 children together.

1951   Opened Walton's Five & Dime in Bentonville, Arkansas.

1962   On July 2 he opened his first Wal-Mart in Rogers, AR.

1970   Wal-Mart stock first traded as publicly-held company.

1971   First 100% Walmart stock split.

1979   First Walmart billion-dollar year in total sales.

1983   The first Sam's Club was opened in Midwest City, OK.

1983   First one hour photo lab opened in Tulsa, Oklahoma.

1983   The "People Greeter" program introduced in all stores.

1984   Mr. Sam does a hula dance on Wall Street to settle a bet.

1985   Mr. Sam named richest man in America by Forbes.

1988   First Supercenter opened in Washington, Missouri.

1991   Walmart becomes America's #1 retailer.

1991   Opens first international store in Mexico City.

1992   Died in Little Rock, Arkansas on April 5.

⌒*About Michael Bergdahl*⌒

$\mathcal{A}$ professional international business speaker, author and turnaround specialist, Michael Bergdahl was the Director of "People" for Wal-Mart in their Bentonville, Arkansas home office. He worked directly with Wal-Mart's founder Sam Walton. Previously he worked in the FMCG Industry for PepsiCo's Frito-Lay Division in the sales organization and headquarters staff assignments. He is also a turnaround specialist who participated in two successful business turnarounds as a VP Human Resources (HR). His 25-year HR background with public companies — PepsiCo, Wal-Mart, Waste Management, and American Eagle Outfitters — spans a variety of industries: Publishing, Petro-Chemical, Consumer Packaged Goods, Discount Retailing, Specialty Retailing, and Solid Waste Industries.

Bergdahl is the author of two books. His first, *WHAT I LEARNED FROM SAM WALTON: How to Compete and Thrive in a Wal-Mart* World (Wiley, 2006) explains the strategies of the world's largest company. The second, *THE 10 RULES OF SAM WALTON: Success Secrets for Remarkable Results* (Wiley, 2008)—with a Foreword by Wal-Mart Chairman Rob Walton, Sam Walton's son—describes the tactics of the world's richest man. Both books are available throughout the world in English as well as Spanish, Russian, Simplified

Chinese, Traditional Chinese, Thai, Indonesian, Korean, and Vietnamese editions.

Michael Bergdahl is considered to be an authority on the best practices of Wal-Mart and Sam Walton.. He has appeared on CNN, CNBC, CNN FN, MSNBC, CNN International, Univision, CBS National Radio and Bloomberg TV. He has participated in internationally televised news debates on "Power Lunch", "On the Money", "Morning Call", and "Closing Bell". Articles written by him, and articles written by others about him, have appeared in business newspapers and magazines around the world. Bergdahl is the moderator of a LinkedIn discussion group called, "Wal-Mart's Best Practices – Super Group" with more than 5000 worldwide members including: Retailers, FMCG Product Manufacturers/Suppliers, and Supply Chain Professionals.

Professional International Speaker

He has spoken professionally in cities on six continents including: * Brisbane, Australia * Beijing, China * Melbourne, Australia * Vancouver, British Columbia * Port of Jiddah, Saudi Arabia * Toronto, Ontario * Caracas, Venezuela * Bogotá, Colombia * Panama City, Panama * Cologne, Germany * Istanbul, Turkey * Malaga, Spain * Moscow, Russia * Port Douglas, Australia * Santiago, Chile * Durban, South Africa * Kiev, Ukraine * Mont Tremblant, Quebec * Valladolid, Spain * Skopje, Macedonia * Belgrade, Serbia * Jeddah, Saudi, Arabia * Dubai, United

Arab Emirates * Kuala Lumpur, Malaysia * Cape Town, South Africa * Guayaquil, Ecuador * Cancun, Mexico * Oslo, Norway * and across the USA *.

Speeches, Master Classes, & Workshops

Michael Bergdahl is a professional international business speaker with substance, who is one part business, one part inspiration, and one part storyteller. He customizes his speeches or workshops to fit the conference theme, and he designs his messages to teach others the Best Practices of Wal-Mart. He presents Keynote Speeches, half day programs, and full day "Master Classes". In his speech, "Growing Your Business the Sam Walton and Wal-Mart Way" (a.k.a. Picking Wal-Mart's POCKETS), Bergdahl unveils the best practices of Wal-Mart, and the success secrets of Sam Walton. Audience members will learn the "Tactics of the World's Richest Man", Sam Walton", and the "Strategies of Wal-Mart, the World's Largest Company."

His Audiences

Michael Bergdahl has spoken at association and business conferences, in the USA and Internationally to Retailers, Non-Retailers, Manufacturers and Suppliers. He speaks to a wide variety of audiences including Sales, Customer Service, IT, Supply Chain/Logistics, Franchisees,

Financial Services, Real Estate Developers, Property Managers, Leasing Agents, Retail Managers, Brand/Marketing Professionals, Human Resources, Plant Managers, Engineers, DC Managers, Operations Managers, Product Manufacturers / Suppliers / Buyers, Pharmacists, Bankers, Credit Union Directors, Presidents, Entrepreneurs, College Professors and College Students, CEO's, CIO's, CTO's, and CFO's. He has spoken at events for Wal-Mart's current suppliers, and its direct competitors, who are interested in improving their ability to compete successfully in a Wal-Mart World!

Be sure to visit Michael online!
www.MichaelBergdahl.net

CPSIA information can be obtained
at www.ICGtesting.com
Printed in the USA
BVOW10s1944080816
458168BV00009BA/152/P

9 781936 587483